Tunes for Ten Fingers

A first piano book for young beginners

by

Pauline Hall

Illustrations by Caroline Crossland

First Published 1981

New Edition © Oxford University Press 1992

Reprinted with corrections 1993.

Reprinted 2023

To the Teacher

This book is intended for the very young beginner.

- One note is introduced at a time.
- Words are used as a natural way of learning rhythm.
- To help rhythmical playing, words longer than a crotchet have oblique dashes after them, corresponding to the length of the note. This ceases after page 38.
- Fingering has been kept to a minimum, and it is left to the teacher to pencil in extra fingering where it is felt to be helpful.
- Great importance is attached to the correct position of the hands; good habits are formed at this stage and the foundations of good technique are laid.
- Finally, learning the piano should be fun. It is hoped that this book will help to make it so.

NOTE: In *Kumbaya* on page 27 the ♩. ♪ rhythm may be used where shown. At this stage no detailed explanation need be given, merely the information that the first crotchet has been lengthened and the second shortened.

Are you ready to play the piano?

Before you start to play, it is a good idea to be able to find your way around the keyboard.

Here are some music games to start you off.

Did you notice that the black keys are grouped in twos and threes?

Play all the groups of three black keys.  Quick as you can!

Play all the groups of two black keys.  Well done!

On the piano there are low sounds and high sounds.

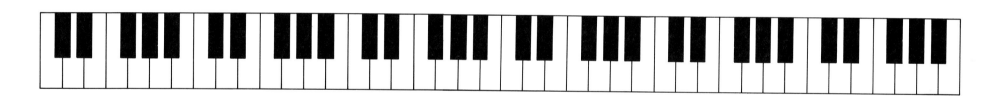

Choose a low-down note and play 'Daddy Bear, are you there?'

On a middle note play 'Mummy Bear, are you there?'

On a high-up note play 'Baby Bear, are you there?'

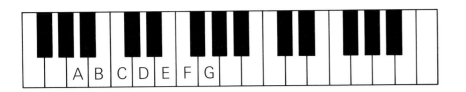

The white keys are called A B C D E F G. These seven letters are repeated right up the piano. Write in the next A B C D E F G on the picture of the piano keyboard.

C is an important note. It is just to the left of the two black keys. Can you find all the Cs on the piano? The C nearest to the middle of the keyboard is called **Middle C**.

Ds are easy! They're in between the two black keys. Hop on to all the Ds.
What about the Es? Can you find them?
Now Fs. Then Gs (a bit more tricky).
Last of all — As and Bs. Now you've played them all!

Try playing some musical words. (The piano picture will help you.)

EGG

BED

BAG

BADGE

Things you need to know before you begin

Music moves with a steady tick like a clock. Each tick of the clock is called a **count** or **beat**.

○   This is a 4-count note. It is held on while you count 1–2–3–4.

♩   This is a 2-count note. It is held on while you count 1–2.

♩   This is a 1-count note. It is held on while you count 1.

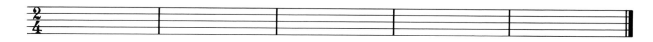

These boxes are called **bars**, and the top number at the beginning tells you how many counts there are in each.

Choose any key and one finger. Can you play this?

Twin - kle,   twin - kle,   lit - tle   star,   How   I   won - der   what   you   are.

And try this:

I   like   mice,   I   think they're nice!

Music notes are written on two ladders.

 (a **treble clef**) shows which is the right-hand ladder.

 (a **bass clef**) shows which is the left-hand ladder.

Middle C sits on its own little line, between the two ladders.

Every note on the keyboard has its own line or space on the music ladder.

This note is on a line.　　　This note is in a space.

Getting ready to play

Keep your hand in the shape of a bridge with your fingers curved and on their tips. Your thumb is part of the bridge, so let it lie on the key.

Could a little mouse sit under your bridge?

Your first right-hand note: Middle C

Middle C sits on its own little line underneath the right-hand ladder.

Play middle C with your right thumb.

I am C! / Mid - dle C! / I can now play mid - dle C! /

Lis - ten to my right hand play, / This must be my luck - y day! /

Mid - dle C's a lit - tle cat, / Purr - ing quiet - ly on the mat! /

Draw some middle Cs here.

Find all the Cs on the piano.

A duet: The sea

Count 4 in each bar. Play the bit about the big waves loudly, and the ripple bit quietly.

Your first left-hand note: Middle C

Something to notice: Middle C for your left hand sits on its own little line above the top of the left-hand ladder.

Play middle C with your left thumb.

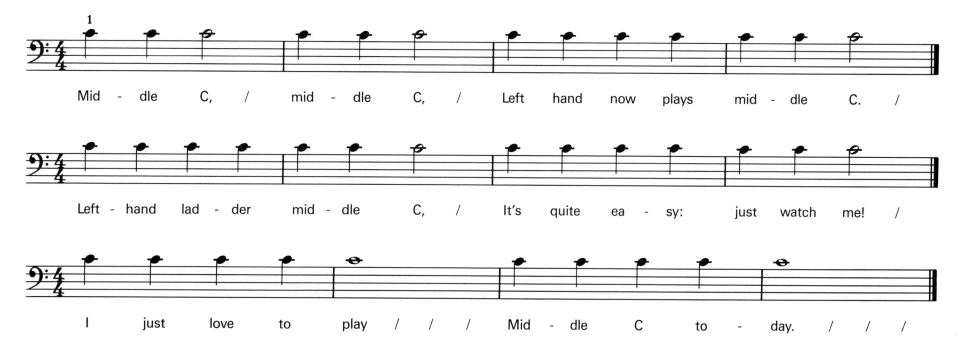

Mid - dle C, / mid - dle C, / Left hand now plays mid - dle C. /

Left - hand lad - der mid - dle C, / It's quite ea - sy: just watch me! /

I just love to play / / / Mid - dle C to - day. / / /

Don't forget to hold on the 4-count middle C.
Hold the key down lightly while you count 1, 2, 3, 4.

𝗈 This is a 4-count note. Draw another one here.

𝅗𝅥 This is a 2-count note. Draw another one here.

♩ This is a 1-count note. Draw another one here.

Your fingers have numbers. Thumbs are 1; write in the others.

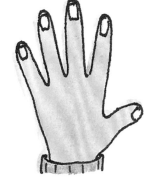

This is your left hand.

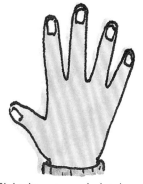

This is your right hand.

New right-hand note: D

D sits underneath the first line. It is a step up from Middle C.

Play D with your 2nd finger.

Dog - gy   D   is   quite   near   C,   /   Just   a   step   a - bove,   you   see.   /

Another tune for D

Dog - gy   D   is   not   a - lone,   /   He   has   got   a   great   big   bone.   /

Find all the other Ds on the piano.
Draw some 4-count Ds. Make sure they
are just below the bottom line.

Try walking your thumb and 2nd finger up and down from C to D, until your fingers know the way.

Sometimes the finger numbers are above the notes to help you.

Dog - gy   D   has   gone   to   sea,   /   He'll   come   back   to   you   and   me.   /

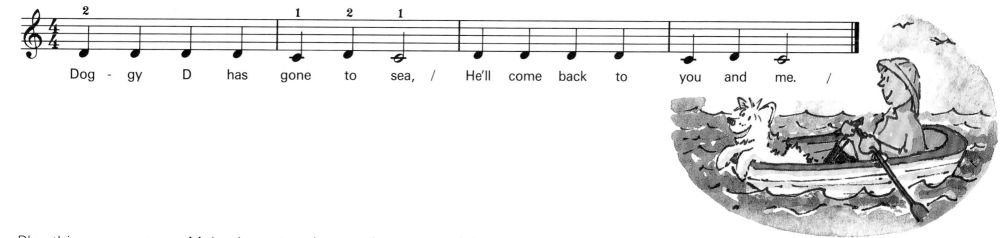

Play this see-saw tune. Make the notes change places up and down very smoothly. Use your thumb for C and 2nd finger for D.

See - saw,   see - saw   up   and   down,   /   See - saw,   see - saw   up   and   down.   /

Dog - gy   D   is   not   a - sleep,   /   He   is   bus - y   count - ing   sheep.   /

New left-hand note: B

B sits up above the top of the left-hand ladder, just a step lower down than Middle C.

Play B with your 2nd finger.

See - saw, see - saw up and down, / C is up and B is down. /

Bum - ble - B! / buzz, buzz, buzz! / How I won - der why he does! /

Bum - ble - B can work for hours / Mak - ing hon - ey out of flowers. /

Find all the Bs on the piano.
Draw some 2-count Bs.
The stalks go down on the left-hand ladder.

Some more tunes for your left hand

Big   Blue - bot - tle,   Bum - ble - Bee,   But - ter - fly   and   Mid - dle   C.   /

When   the   weath - er's   hot   and   sun - ny,   Bum - ble   Bee   likes   mak - ing   hon - ey.

A duet: Marching

March - ing,   march - ing   down   the   street, /   Hear   the   tramp   of   sold - iers'   feet! /

Accompaniment

Right hand plays C and D with fingers 1 and 2.
Left hand plays C and B with fingers 1 and 2.

Mid-dle C and Dog-gy D, / play-ing in the sun, / / / Mid-dle C and Bum-ble Bee, / hav-ing lots of fun. / / /

Keep your hand in the shape of a bridge when you play. Don't let your fingers go flat.

See - saw, see - saw, left hand likes to see - saw, see - saw up and down.

Left hand plays a see-saw tune. The notes change places smoothly without any gaps in between.

Tunes for right hand and left hand

The Rocking Chair

Make this tune sound smooth and rocking. Play it rather slowly.

Rock-ing, rock-ing   to and fro, / Rock-ing up and down I go. / I just love to   rock all day / In my rock-ing   chair.///

A duet: The Grandfather Clock

Look carefully to see which hand plays, and be ready to change over. Count 1-2-3-4 on each note.

Accompaniment

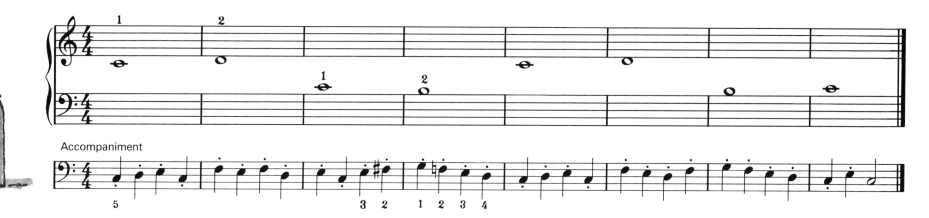

New right-hand note: E

E sits on the first line of the ladder, just above D.

Play E with your 3rd finger.

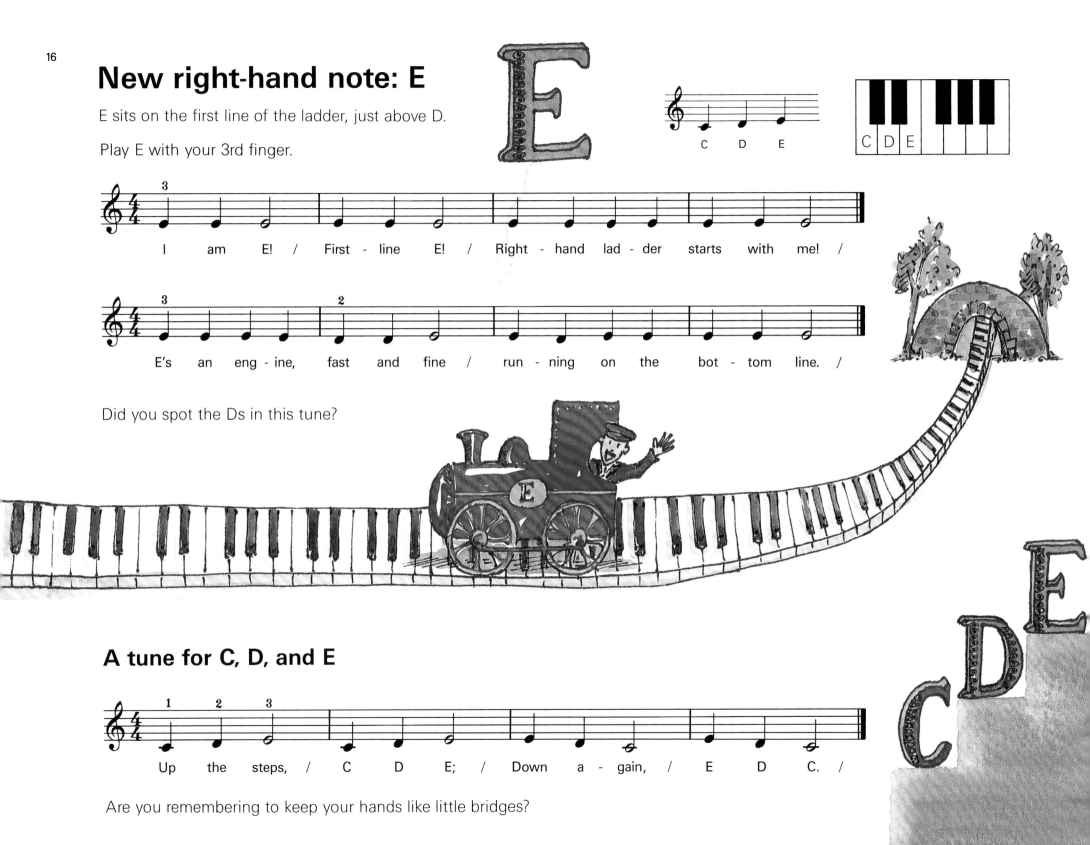

I am E! / First-line E! / Right-hand lad-der starts with me! /

E's an eng-ine, fast and fine / run-ning on the bot-tom line. /

Did you spot the Ds in this tune?

A tune for C, D, and E

Up the steps, / C D E; / Down a-gain, / E D C. /

Are you remembering to keep your hands like little bridges?

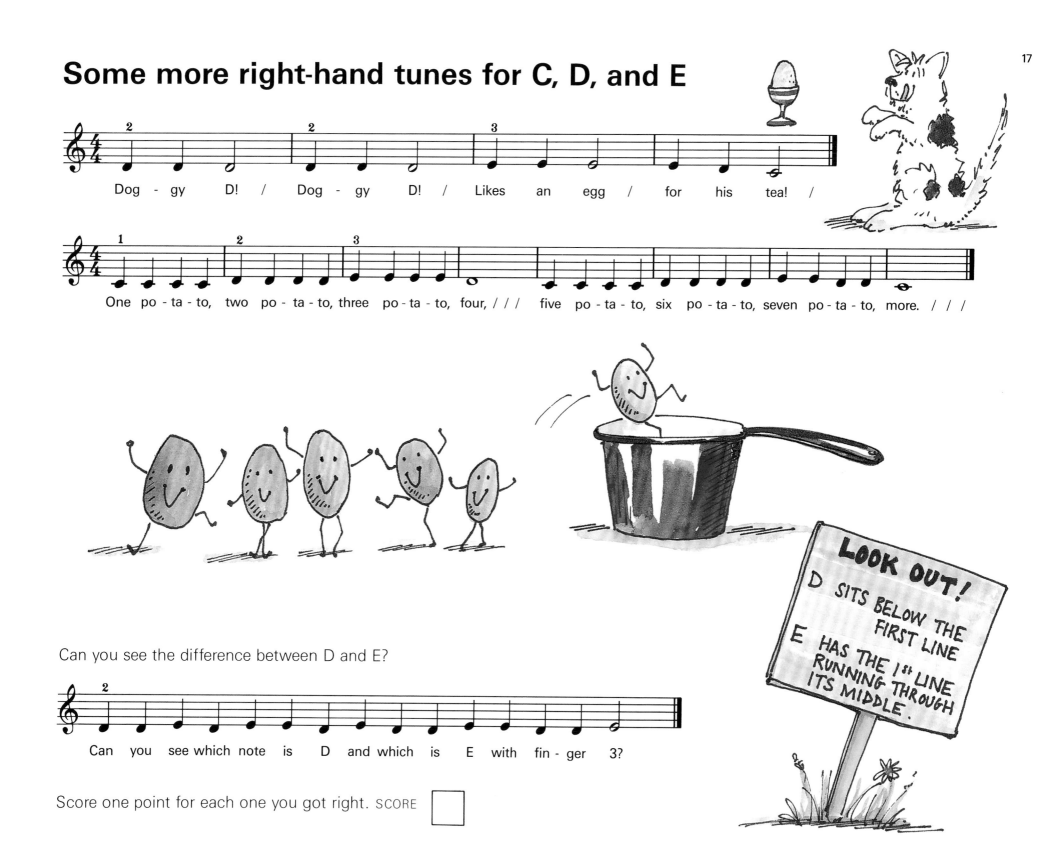

Some more right-hand tunes for C, D, and E

Dog - gy D! / Dog - gy D! / Likes an egg / for his tea! /

One po - ta - to, two po - ta - to, three po - ta - to, four, / / / five po - ta - to, six po - ta - to, seven po - ta - to, more. / / /

Can you see the difference between D and E?

Can you see which note is D and which is E with fin - ger 3?

Score one point for each one you got right. SCORE

LOOK OUT!
D SITS BELOW THE FIRST LINE
E HAS THE 1st LINE RUNNING THROUGH ITS MIDDLE.

To remind you

○   A fat note without a stalk is worth 4 counts.
Its real name is a SEMIBREVE (or WHOLE NOTE).

♩   A fat note with a stalk going up or down is worth 2 counts.
Its real name is a MINIM (or HALF NOTE).

♩   A black note like a tadpole is worth 1 count.
Its real name is a CROTCHET (or QUARTER NOTE).

This is the right-hand ladder.
The curly sign is a **treble clef.**

This is the left-hand ladder.
The sign like a back-to-front C
is a **bass clef**.

These boxes are called bars. The top figure at the beginning tells you how many counts there are in each bar. (Don't bother about the lower figure.)

A new kind of note

♩.   A 2-count note with a dot is worth 3 counts.

Elephants' Waltz

Make this tune really dance along.

These dots mean 'Play it again.'

Duet part

More right-hand tunes for C, D, and E

This tune has 3 counts to each bar.

See! / / See! / / What do I see? / / Two / black beet-les and one / fat flea! / /

E-le-phant E! / / E-le-phant E! / / Fell from the top of a sy-ca-more tree. / /

Write the names of the notes underneath them.

Mary had a Little Lamb

Mar - y had a lit - tle lamb,/ lit - tle lamb,/ lit - tle lamb. / Mar - y had a lit - tle lamb, its fleece was white as snow. / / /

Little Arabella Miller

Lit - tle A - ra - bel - la Mil - ler found a wool - ly ca - ter - pil - lar.

Find all the Es on the piano.

Play next-door notes with next-door fingers. When you miss a note out, miss a finger out too!

New left-hand note: A

A sits on the top line of the left-hand ladder.

Play A with your 3rd finger.

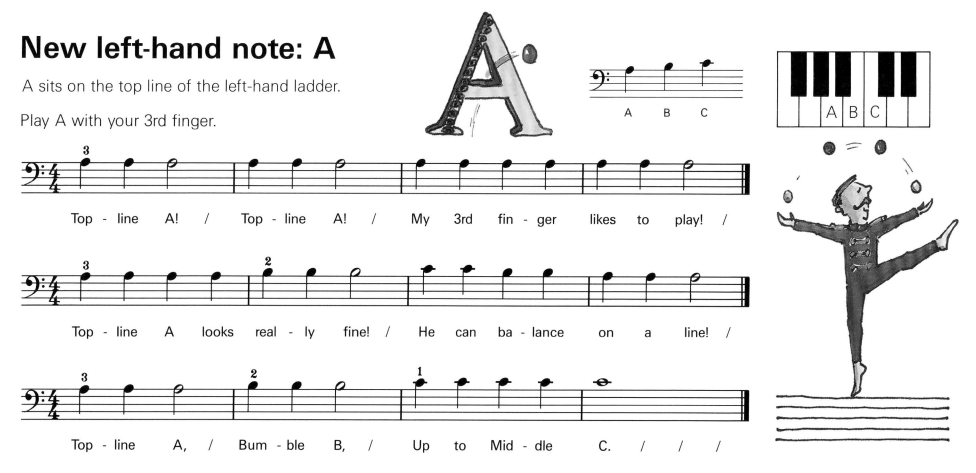

Top - line   A!   /   Top - line   A!   /   My   3rd   fin - ger   likes   to   play!   /

Top - line   A   looks   real - ly   fine!   /   He   can   ba - lance   on   a   line!   /

Top - line   A,   /   Bum - ble   B,   /   Up   to   Mid - dle   C.   /   /   /

Find all the As on the piano.
Draw some 3-count As. Don't forget —
the top line goes through their middle.

Some music games

Blind Man's Buff

How good are you at FEELING your way about the piano? Shut your eyes, and your teacher will tell you what to find.

In between each note, you must put your hands on your knees.

Find: 1. A group of three black keys

2. A group of two black keys

3. A white key in between two black keys

4. Any C

5. Another C

6. An E, low-down towards the bottom of the keyboard

7. A high-up E, towards the top of the keyboard

Guess the Note

Play any note near the middle of the piano. Then sing it. Play the note again.

Was your sung note the same as the piano note?

Stepping Stones

Can you cross the river? Each stone has a note on it. Write the number of counts beside each one.

Then count as you jump from stone to stone.

THINK BEFORE YOU JUMP!

New right-hand note: F

F sits in the first space of the right-hand ladder.

Play F with your 4th finger.

C   D   E   F

C D E F

F's a fat and fool - ish frog, / Sit - ting on a moss - y log. /

F is sit - ting in a space, / Has a smile up - on his face. /

Walk up to F, / / Walk back a - gain. / /

Draw some 4-count Fs. Don't make your notes too fat — they must squeeze between two lines!

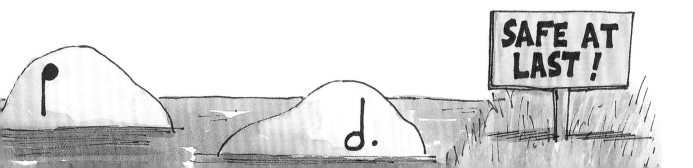

Some more tunes for F

Frank Frog

F's a frog, his name is Frank, / Lives be - side the ri - ver bank. /

A Surprise

Un - der - neath the gar - den shed / Four black rab - bits are in bed. /

Can you see the difference?

E is on a line

F is in a space

Rabbits' Lullaby

Play this very quietly

Sweet - ly sleep, / Lul - la - by, / Stars are twink - ling in the sky. /

Duet part

New left-hand note: G

G sits in the top space of the left-hand ladder, just below top-line A. Play G with your 4th finger.

G's a grum-py gar-den gnome,/ Sit-ting in his flower-bed home./

Grum-py G, / Top-line A, / Bum-ble B, / Mid-dle C. /

My wish

I wish I was a lit-tle grub with whisk-ers round my tum-my; / I'd

climb in-to a ho-ney-pot and make my tum-my gum-my! /

Tunes for left and right hand

Yankee Doodle

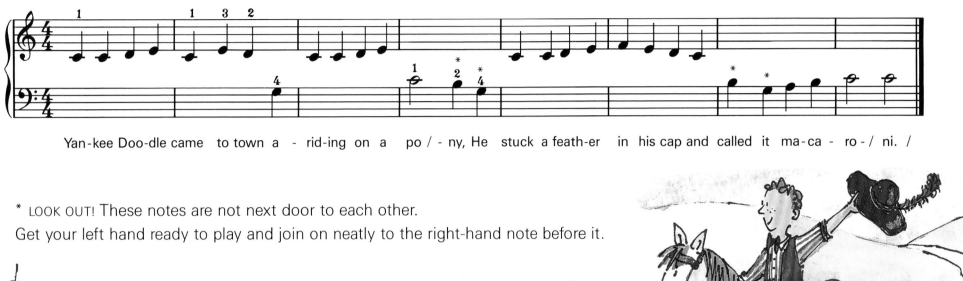

Yan-kee Doo-dle came to town a - rid-ing on a po / - ny, He stuck a feath-er in his cap and called it ma-ca-ro-/ni. /

* LOOK OUT! These notes are not next door to each other.
Get your left hand ready to play and join on neatly to the right-hand note before it.

Westminster Chimes

Count 1, 2, 3 steadily. Remember to hold each 𝅗𝅥., which lasts 3 counts.

Kumbaya

Verse 1: Kum - ba - ya my Lord, / Kum - ba ya, / / / Kum - ba - ya my Lord, / Kum - ba - ya, / / /
Verse 2: Some - one's sing - ing, Lord. . .
Verse 3: Some - one's pray - ing, Lord. . .

Do you remember what these dots mean?
If not, have a look on page 18.

Kum - ba - ya my Lord, / Kum - ba - ya, / / Oh Lord, Kum - ba - ya. / / /

* See 'To the Teacher'

'Kumbaya' means 'Come by here'.

Old MacDonald had a Farm

Old Mac-Donald had a farm,/ E I E I O!/ / And on that farm he had some ducks,/ E I E I O!/ / /

Quack, quack here,/ Quack, quack there,/ Everywhere a quack, quack, quack!/ Old Mac-Donald had a farm,/ E I E I O!/ / /

Only three notes are needed for
your left hand: C, G, and A.

The Haunted House

(by Helen Moncur aged 7, who wrote the words too)

Creep - ing through the haunt - ed house / Went a lit - tle tin - y mouse. /

Saw some ghosts and gob - lin hosts / In that creep - y haunt - ed house. /

Play this quietly and make it sound very creepy and ghostly.
Join your hands neatly when they change.

New right-hand note: G

G sits on the 2nd line of the right-hand ladder.

Play G with your 5th finger.

Second line G, / / Play it and see! / /

George

George is my guin - ea - pig, lives in his hutch. / /

He likes my play - ing, but not ve - ry much! / /

Can you see the difference?

E on the first line

and

G on the second line

Cuck - oo!

A Christmas Carol
Good King Wenceslas

Good King Wen - ces - las looked out / On the feast of Ste / - phen, / When the snow lay

round a - bout, / Deep and crisp and ev / - en: / Bright - ly shone the moon that night, / Tho' the frost was

cru / - el, / When a poor man came in sight, / Gath'r - ing win - ter fu - / / / / - el. / / /

32

When two notes on the same line or in the same space are joined like this ♩‿♩ the curve between them is called a **tie**.

They look as if they were tied together with a piece of string.
Play the first note and count it. Hold it on while you count the second note as well.

1 2 3 4 + 1 2   1 2 + 1   1 2 3 + 1 2

Count 1, 2 in a bar. Look out for the tied notes, and hold the second one on.

Little Miss Muffet

Your left hand plays only the last two notes.

Little Bo Peep

Lit - tle Bo Peep / has lost / her sheep / And does-n't know where __ to find / / them. / /

Leave them a - lone / and they'll / come home, / / Bring - ing their tails __ be - hind / / them. / /

Twinkle, Twinkle, little Star

Play this quite quietly.
Join on neatly when one hand takes over from the other.

Twin - kle, twin - kle, lit - tle star, / How I won - der what you are, / Up a-bove the world so high, /

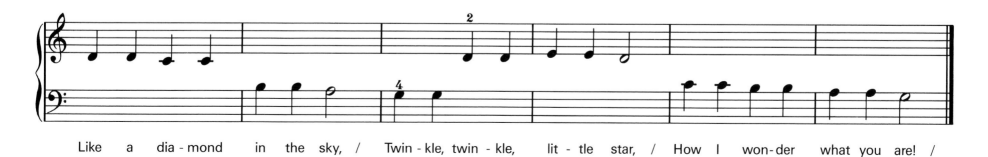

Like a dia - mond in the sky, / Twin - kle, twin - kle, lit - tle star, / How I won - der what you are! /

34

Bluebird

Blue - bird, blue-bird, on my shoul-der, Blue-bird, blue-bird, on my shoul-der, Blue - bird, blue - bird, on my shoul-der,

on a sum - mer morn / - ing. /

Keep your hands ready
to play their share of the tune.

Duet part

To have a bluebird on your shoulder is another way of saying you feel happy.

A duet: Cowboy Joe

Your right hand plays the tune.
Play this quite slowly.

Cow - boy Joe from Mex - i - co / gail - y rides a - long, / / / As he swings a - cross the plain he

sings a hap - py song, / hap - py song, / hap - py song. / / / / / / /

Accompaniment — left hand plays notes with stems down.

(R.H.)

(L.H.)

New left-hand note: F

Look out for left-hand F.
Is it on a line or in a space?

Play F with your 5th finger.

F   G   A   B   C

5

Fire - man Fred's a   friend of   mine, /   ba - lan - cing   up - on   a   line.

3 **4** **5** **3** **5** **4**

Top - line   A   and   down to   F, /   Now   I   know the   way. / / /   Go - ing   up, /   go - ing down: /   ea - sy   tune to   play. / / /

Look out! Here comes the fire-engine!
Let your 5th and 4th fingers make the sound of a fire-engine, like this:

5 **4**

(Good exercise for that little finger!)

Five little monkeys

5 **4** **3** **5** **4**

Five /   lit - tle   mon /- keys, /   play - ing   in the   sun; / / /   Tea - sing Un - cle   Cro - co - dile, /   ha - ving lots of   fun. / / /

A tune for all the notes you know

Right Hand

Left Hand

F G A B C C C D E F G

Fire-man F, / Grum-py G, / Top-line A, and Bum-ble B. / Mid-dle C, / Shag-gy Dog, / Engine E, and Fool-ish Frog. /

Guin-ea-pig and right-hand G: / All go back to Mid-dle C. /

Your hands play together in the last bar but one.

A duet: Soft and Loud

Start this tune very quietly and make it get gradually louder and louder as the band gets nearer.

The musical sign for getting louder is

Rests

A **rest** is a silent count.

 or   This is a rest worth ♩ or one count.

This is a rest worth 𝅗𝅥 or two counts.
It looks like a little black brick on top of the third line.

This is a rest worth 𝅝 or four counts.
It hangs down from the fourth line.

In these tunes say 'ssh!' in each rest.

Pretend you are a cuckoo.

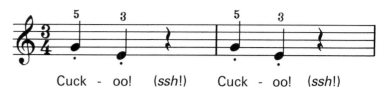

Cuck - oo!   (ssh!)   Cuck - oo!   (ssh!)

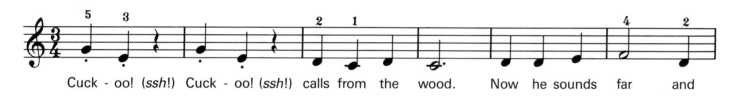

Cuckoo

Cuck - oo! (ssh!) Cuck - oo! (ssh!) calls from the wood.   Now he sounds far and

now he sounds near.   (ssh!)   Cuck - oo! (ssh!)   Cuck - oo! (ssh!)   spring - time is here.

Are you remembering to keep your hand in a nice bridge-shape? Fingers curved and on their tips.

Make the notes with dots underneath them short and jumpy. Don't forget the rests.

Quavers

♪♪ these twin notes are called **quavers.**

The twins are worth one ♩ called a **crotchet.**

One quaver on its own looks like this: ♪

Say and clap at the same time:

> Baa baa black sheep, have you any wool?
> Yes sir, yes sir, three bags full;
> One for the master, one for the dame,
> One for the little boy who lives down the lane.

Did you spot where the quavers came?
Here is *Baa baa black sheep* in notes.
Clap it:

Now you know five notes for your right hand and five for your left hand, so you can play all these tunes.

F G A B C

C D E F G

Jingle Bells

Jin - gle bells,   jin - gle bells,   jin - gle all the way,   Oh what fun it is to ride in a one horse o - pen

sleigh!   Oh,   Jin - gle bells,   jin - gle bells,   jin - gle all the way,   Oh what fun it is to ride in a

one horse o - pen sleigh!

Look out for the quavers.
They come on the words 'in a'.
They must fit exactly into 1 count.

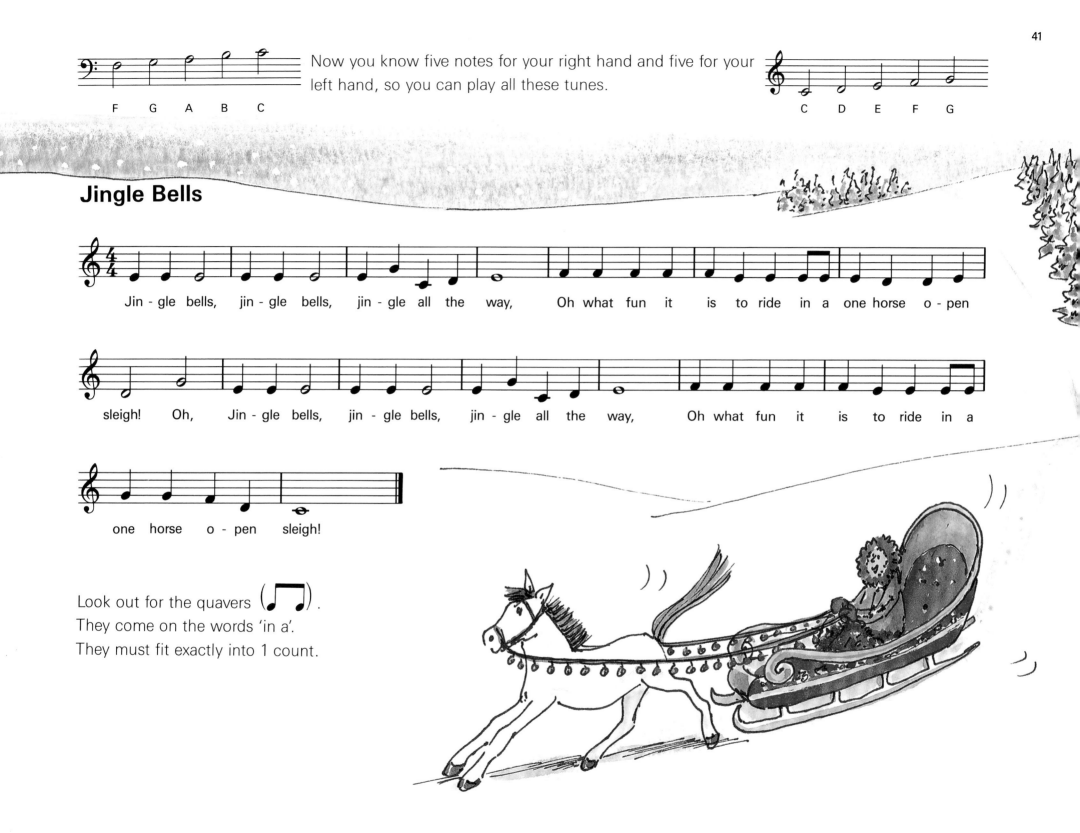

Two little Dicky-birds

This tune has a lot of quavers in it.
Two quavers must fit neatly into 1 count.

Two lit - tle dicky-birds   sit - ting on   a wall,   One called   Pe - ter,   one called   Paul.   Fly   a-way   Pe - ter,

fly   a - way   Paul,   Come   back   Pe - ter,   come   back   Paul!

Tinker, Tailor

For your left hand

Tin - ker,   tail - or,   sold - ier,   sail - or,   Rich   man, poor   man,   beg - gar - man, thief!

This Old Man

This old man, he played one, He played nick nack on my drum, Nick nack pad-dy-wack,

give a dog a bone, This old man came roll-ing home!

Clap:

Nick nack pad-dy-wack! Nick nack pad-dy-wack!

Walking

Walk-ing, walk-ing down the hill, then run-ning up and down a-gain to C.

Hush, Little Baby

Slowly and quietly

Hush, lit - tle ba - by   don't say a word,   Papa's gon - na buy you a mock - ing bird.   If that mock - ing

bird don't sing,   Pa-pa's gon-na buy you a   dia - mond ring!

Happy Birthday to You

Practise this so that you can play it perfectly on a special birthday.

Hap - py birth - day to you, Hap - py birth - day to you, Hap - py birth - day dear

Mum - my, Hap - py birth - day to you.

Before you play, clap this:

Hap - py birth - day, Hap - py birth - day.

Halloween Night

(by Nicholas Bancroft, who wrote the words too)

Nicholas found that if he played the black key to the left of E instead of E,
it made the music sound more creepy and witch-like.

This note is E flat. This is a flat sign: ♭.

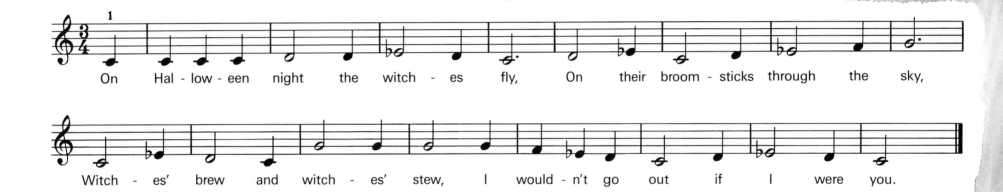

On Hal - low - een night the witch - es fly, On their broom - sticks through the sky,

Witch - es' brew and witch - es' stew, I would - n't go out if I were you.

Two tunes to sing and play

The Princess

1. There was a Prin-cess long a-go, long a-go, long a-go, There was a Prin-cess long a-go, long a-go.

Play the other verses too:

2. She lived inside a castle tall.
3. A wicked fairy cast a spell.
4. The Princess slept a hundred years.
5. A noble Prince came riding by.
6. He woke the Princess from her sleep.
7. The wedding bells rang out with joy.

Skip to my Lou

Choose your part - ner, skip to my Lou, Choose your part - ner,

skip to my Lou, Choose your part - ner, skip to my Lou, Skip to my Lou my dar - ling.

WELL DONE !

Now that you have completed your first book, you can move on to **MORE TUNES FOR TEN FINGERS** !

Could a mouse still sit under your bridge ?